NATIONAL SLOGANS
FROM
AROUND THE WORLD

by
Henry Conserva

HAPPY LANE PUBLISHERS
848 PATTI PAGE CT.
WINDSOR, CA 95492

Bloomington, IN  Milton Keynes, UK

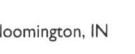

AuthorHouse™
1663 Liberty Drive, Suite 200
Bloomington, IN 47403
www.authorhouse.com
Phone: 1-800-839-8640

AuthorHouse™ UK Ltd.
500 Avebury Boulevard
Central Milton Keynes, MK9 2BE
www.authorhouse.co.uk
Phone: 08001974150

First published by AuthorHouse 5/30/2006

ISBN: 1-4259-2987-7 (sc)

Library of Congress Control Number: 2006904493

*Printed in the United States of America
Bloomington, Indiana*

This book is printed on acid-free paper.

TABLE OF CONTENTS

ARMENIA...1

BRAZIL 2

CANADA..3

CHILE 4

CHINA 6

CROATIA 9

DENMARK 11

DOMINICA 12

EGYPT...13

ESTONIA 14

ETHIOPIA..15

FINLAND 16

FRANCE...17

GERMANY 19

GREECE 22

ICELAND..23

INDIA...24

INDONESIA 25

IRELAND... 26

ISRAEL 28

ITALY... 30

JAPAN..33

LEBANON..35

LUXEMBOURG 36

MEXICO 37

NORWAY...38

POLAND 39

PORTUGAL 40

RUSSIA 41

SAUDI ARABIA 43

SPAIN 44

SWEDEN..45

TRINIDAD AND TOBAGO 46

TURKEY 48

UNITED KINGDOM 49

THE UNITED STATES OF AMERICA 51

VIETNAM...56

ZIMBABWE 58

INTRODUCTION

As a high school history teacher, I developed an interest in slogans from showing my students documentary films on World War II subjects. I felt sick to my stomach upon seeing a slogan on a Nazi death camp gate which read "Arbeit macht Frei" (Work makes you free). The hope implied in the slogan never materialized for the countless inmates who had to face hell on earth. I tried investigating slogans of various nations but I never seemed to get very far. I had great difficulty finding much in the way of published works on the subject. After I retired I made up my mind to take a direct approach and write to embassies in Washington, D.C. as well as consulates in San Francisco, California. Not all the embassies and consulates contacted responded but those who did were generous in sharing their knowledge of slogans with me and for that I am grateful.

The word slogan most likely originated as a battle cry of ancient Scottish or Irish warriors. It is defined as a phrase expressing the aims of nature of an enterprise or organization. The word motto is a synonym for slogan. A slogan is an abbreviated idea which, hopefully, will persuade people to think as you want them to think.

One of the most persistent human efforts is for elite groups in any society to try to persuade, brainwash, those members of society lower on the social class structure to think or act in a desired way. What better way to do this than to create an oversimplified easily remembered statement.

Slogans are not designed to be carefully examined but to be accepted without question. Slogans can be very short-lived or long-lived. They can be as short as one word or as long as a brief paragraph. Some are catchy while others are plain and straightforward.

There are several categories of slogans. One of the most common and pervasive is found in the world of commercial advertising. Advertising is the driving force behind the stimulation and increase in consumption of goods and services in our business-orientated world. Examples of slogans such General Electric's "Progress is our most important product" and Buick's "The road belongs to Buick" each had a fairly long run in the mass media.

Each one of America's fifty states has a state motto. They can constitute a single word such as California's "Eureka" (I've found it) or the "Friendship" motto of the state of Texas or they can be rather lengthy. Hawaii's "The life of the land if perpetuated by righteousness" or Missouri's "Salus Populi Suprema Esto" (the welfare of the people shall be the supreme law) are fairly long mottos.

Clubs, social organizations and schools, universities and colleges all have their slogans. Harvard's "Veritas" (Truth) comes to mind as one of many old school slogans.

I have chosen national slogans as the subject of this book. As I have said before, I wrote to embassies and consulates and the core of my work is based on their responses. The slogans are listed by country and, since each national slogan has its own unique history, I've provided some background information.

National slogans have been put to many uses. I've identified a few of them. Many national slogans reflect the cultural values of their respective nations. France's "Liberty, Equality, Fraternity" is an example as is Israel's "Peace with security."

Sometimes a nation's expansionist ambitions will be revealed in a slogan. In the mid-nineteenth century, the United States had people in political parades shouting "Fifty-four forty or fight!" This slogan reflected a goal of President James K. Polk to gain land in the Oregon Country from Great Britain. In Nazi Germany the slogan "Heute gehort uns Deutschland und morgen die ganze welt' (Today we have Germany, tomorrow the whole world) seemed to leave little doubt as to the intentions of Adolf Hitler.

One type of national slogan comes as a statement that constitutes a threat. In colonial America on the eve of a revolution "Don't tread on me!" was printed on flags as a warning to the British to be careful in their dealings with the colonists. Chile's "By right or by might" seems somewhat aggressive and threatening.

Many national slogans are affirmations of commitment to a nation or its people. The Norwegian king's "All for Norway" illustrates this slogan type as does Ireland's "Erin go bragh" (Ireland forever).

Nations have sometimes stressed their professed relationship to a supreme being. Germans at various times have stated "Gott sei mit uns" (God be with us) and Americans have placed "In God we trust" on their currency.

National goals other then territorial expansion have often become the subjects for slogans. Japan's "Enrich the country and strengthen the military" clearly states Japan's goals during the Meiji Period (1868-1912). Indonesia's "Merdeka" (Freedom) puts a national goal in the simplest most direct form.

An example of a devious slogan that eventually led to an entrapment of people who carried out its principles was the slogan of Mao's China that stated "let a hundred schools of thought contend and let a hundred flowers blossom". Many artists and writers who did follow the spirit of the slogan and express their true feelings were easily identified as enemies of the state and severely punished.

Some national slogans have been used to develop a cult of personality around certain heads of state. These slogans seldom outlive the people chosen for such acclaim. Nazi Germany's "Heil Hitler" (Hail Hitler) and fascist Italy's "Mussolini ha sempre ragione" (Mussolini is always right) are examples of well known relatively short-lived slogans.

These comments on national slogans are in no way to thought of as complete or definitive, but they do make a starting point for further investigations into the role that national slogans play in human history. Slogans are still being used and the future will undoubtedly see new ones. May they never descend to the level of those portrayed by George Orwell in his book *1984*. In this work speech and thought are controlled by Big Brother and citizens are brainwashed automatons. They lived by the slogans "War is Peace", "Freedom is Slavery", and "Ignorance is Strength."

I feel that this book should be of use to students of history, sociology, advertising, psychology and many other subjects. I can visualize the topic of national slogans as a different way to engage students in a study of other nations as well as our own. Besides this target group I hope that this book will be of interest to the general reader.

ARMENIA

Ancient Armenia extended into parts of what are today Turkey and Iran. Present day Armenia was turned into a Soviet Republic on April 2, 1921 and became a constituent republic of the Union of Soviet Socialist Republics on December 5, 1936.

Armenia declared its independence on September 23, 1991. Among the most popular slogans from the very beginning of the new independent Armenia was "**fight, fight, until the end**". That meant that the aim of the Armenian people was to get free from the Soviet Union by any possible means.

Source:
Embassy of the Republic of Armenia, Washington, D.C.

BRAZIL

In 1807, France invaded Portugal because the Portuguese had supported Great Britain in a war between the French and the British. The ruler of Portugal, Prince John VI, fled Portugal for his colonial city of Rio de Janeiro, Brazil. The city became the capital of the Portuguese Empire in 1808. Prince John VI gave Brazil the status of a kingdom in 1815.

In 1821 the Portuguese royal family returned to Portugal leaving John VI's son, Crown Prince Pedro, to rule Brazil. Pedro had said that "if it is for the well being of all people and happiness of the nation, tell the people that I will stay." In 1822, Pedro proclaimed Brazil an independent constitutional monarchy and had himself crowned Emperor Pedro I. A slogan of this time was **"Independencia ou Morte!"** (Independence or Death). It should be noted that Brazil's freedom was achieved without bloodshed. Portugal officially recognized Brazil's independence in 1825.

Source:
Consulate General of Brazil, San Francisco

CANADA

———————•———————

"The Twentieth Century Belongs to Canada" is a well-known Canadian slogan. The words were spoken by Sir Wilfred Laurier in 1919. The slogan has remained popular with the people of Canada for decades and is viewed as a touchstone of national aspiration measured against national achievement.

Canada is a vast land comprising over 3,849,674 square miles. It is the largest nation in the entire Western Hemisphere. Among Canada's many resources are forests, fisheries and, fine agricultural land and seaports on three coasts as well as the Great Lakes. Mineral wealth includes oil, natural gas, nickel, zinc, copper, gold, lead, molybdenum, potash, silver, iron ore, platinum, sulfur, tungsten, and titanium in addition to many others. It's easy to see why Canadians have such high hopes for the future of their country.

Source:
Canadian Consulate General, Los Angeles

CHILE

The national motto of Chile is "Por la Razon o la Fuerza" which means **"By Right or by Might."** The attitudes behind this slogan were illustrated in the War of the Pacific that started in 1879 and ended in 1883. Peru, Bolivia and Chile were involved in a dispute as to who should rightfully control the nitrate and copper rich Atacama Desert on the west coast of South America. The desert had the world's greatest natural nitrate deposits essential to the manufacture of munitions. Peru and Bolivia signed a secret alliance pact that called for unity in case of offensive acts by other powers. With a breakdown of negotiations between Chile and Bolivia coupled with a Peruvian rejection of neutrality, Chile declared war on its two neighbors on April 5, 1879.

The Chilean ground forces were superior to the combined forces of Bolivia and Peru. Victory followed victory for the Chilean armies. Also she had the best navy among the adversaries and had ironclads among her vessels. She won the war and took the spoils. Chile took possession of all parts of the Atacama Desert that had been owned by Bolivia and Peru, making Bolivia a landlocked nation without a coastline. (Chile later agreed to the building of a railroad from Africa on the coast to the Bolivian capital at La Paz. This gave Bolivia a chance to import and export goods with the world's nations.) Chile had increased its land area by more than a third.

Today the motto is dated and no longer reflects the thinking of Chileans on how to conduct foreign affairs.

Source:
Consul General of Chile, San Francisco

CHINA

China is no stranger to slogans as one can guess about a nation that has existed for thousands of years. The period of Mao Tse-tung brought forth slogans that were both unusual and ruinous in their effects. In May of 1956, Mao made the statement, "Let a hundred schools of thought content and let a hundred flowers blossom." From this statement two slogans emerged. The least controversial was **"Let a hundred schools of thought contend"**, which was designed to let scientists pursue their work without restrictions. The more controversial slogan was **"Let a hundred flowers blossom"** which was aimed at artists and writers.

The "Hundred Flowers" campaign was formally endorsed by the Eighth Party Congress in September 1956. It seems that Mao wanted to experiment with public opinion and find out how the party stood in China. He apparently also wanted to curb the poor practices of some members of the bureaucracy by exposing them to open criticism.

There was considerable opposition to the "Hundred Flowers" campaign within the apparatus of the Chinese Communist Party. Regardless, the policy was carried out. Promises were made of intellectual freedom for artists and writers. They were told that they would have the freedom of independent thought, free discussion and open debate on issues. It was made clear in many pronouncements that opinions could be freely expressed. It is likely that Mao and other party leaders had no idea of how much criticism the party would receive. It wasn't long before outspoken intellectuals were branded as "enemies of socialism" and silenced with force.

Another slogan of the Chinese Communists was the **"Great Leap Forward"** which was conceived in 1958 as a means of propelling China into the front ranks of industrialized nations literally overnight. Actually, the campaign became a great leap backwards for China. Farms were collectivized and millions of Chinese were put to work building water conservation projects and manufacturing steel, often with backyard furnaces.

The plan was not well organized. Slogans such as **"more, better, faster and more economical"** couldn't make the **"Great Leap Forward"** work even if people were promised a **"thousand years of happiness"**. The steel making campaign ended in the spring of 1959. It was a catastrophe. The numbers of people assigned to non-agricultural projects denied the agricultural sector of the economy the necessary labor to adequately feed the population. When the **"Great Leap Forward"** ended in 1961, much of China's economy was shattered.

Sources:

Hoyt, Edwin P. *The Rise of the Chinese Republic: From the Last Emperor to Deng Xiaoping* McGraw-Hill Publishing Co. New York 1989

Meisner, Maurice *Mao's China: A History of the People's Republic* The Free Press New York 1977

Rodinski, Witold *The People's Republic of China: A Concise Political History* The Free Press New York 1988

CROATIA

Croatia is located in southeastern Europe on the Balkan Peninsula. Its neighbors are Slovenia and Hungary to the North with Bosnia, Herzogovina and Yugoslavia to the South. These are three significant Croatian national slogans:

1. "Bog I Hrvati!" (**God and Croats**). This is a slogan from the mid-nineteenth century when Croatia was within the Austro-Hungarian Empire. It was coined by Dr. Ante Starcevic, president of the Croatian Party of Rights, in order to emphasize that only Croats themselves, without any foreign help, can achieve their freedom and independence.

2. **"Vjera u Boga I seljačka sloga!"** (Faith in God and peasants' unity). This slogan was popular during the 1920s, when Croatia was included into newly created Yugoslavia (1918). It was the official motto of the Croatian Peasant Party, proudly led by Dr. Stjepan Radic who was assassinated in Belgrade's Parliament (1928)

3. **"Zna se!"** (One knows! or Everybody knows!). The most recent slogan, meaning: "It is not necessary

to explain who can realize the old Croatian dreams of liberty; it goes without saying," was used by the Croatian Democratic Union during the first democratic elections in former Yugoslavia (1990). The slogan was proposed by party leader Dr. Franjo Tudjman, former President of the Republic of Croatia.

Source:
Embassy of the Republic of Croatia in the United States, Washington, D.C.

DENMARK

A slogan from the Denmark of 1935 is **"Stauning Eller Kaos"** (Stauning or Chaos). The slogan is taken from an election poster. Stauning ran for Prime minister in the 1935 Danish election to the Folketing (Danish Parliament) and won. Stauning was the leader of the Social Democrats. As in many European countries at that time, people wanted a strong man to head the government. One only has to think of Nazi Germany's Hitler, Fascist Italy's Mussolini and Falangist Spain's Franco to find support for this idea. In the 1930s Denmark and indeed most nations in the world were affected by high unemployment and general poverty.

Source:
Royal Danish Embassy, Washington, D.C.

DOMINICA

The Commonwealth of Dominica lies in the Eastern Caribbean and is the most northerly of the Windward Islands. Its neighbors are Guadeloupe to the North and Martinique to the South.

A slogan from the recent history of Dominica is **"Fear no more."** This slogan was used by a newly formed political party for contesting two consecutive election campaigns. The party won the second campaign and formed the elected government.

Dominica only achieved political independence from Great Britain in 1978. The Freedom Party held power from 1980 to 1995. A new party, the United Workers Party, was formed in 1988, two years before it took part in its first election contest. The slogan **"Fear no more"** was deemed appropriate because most of the citizens felt a degree of fear in expressing their feelings freely. The slogan became very powerful and was used again during the campaign of 1995. The United Workers' Party is currently the government of the Commonwealth of Dominica.

Source:
Embassy of the Commonwealth of Dominica.

EGYPT

———————•———————

A slogan from Egypt figured in the October War (1973) after which Egypt regained land it had previously lost to Israel. In Arabic the slogan reads

" ما أخذ بالقوة لايسترد بغير القوة "

which means "What was taken by force should be regained by force. In October 1973 a full-scale war erupted between Israel and the Arab nations of Egypt and Syria. During the fighting, Egyptian troops regained some of Egypt's territory in the Sinai Peninsula. A cease-fire ended the fighting between Egypt and Israel in November 1973. The two nations agreed to a separation of their forces in the Sinai in 1974. In 1975, they reached an agreement under which Israel removed its troops from a part of the Sinai that it had occupied since 1967. In 1978 Israel agreed to withdraw from the Sinai altogether.

Source:
Embassy of the Arab Republic of Egypt

ESTONIA

Estonia lies in Eastern Europe bordering the Baltic Sea and the Gulf of Finland. Estonia's neighbors are Russia on the East and Latvia on the South. Estonia was a province of Imperial Russia before World War I. It achieved independence between World War I and II. In 1940 Estonia was conquered by the Union of Soviet Socialist Republics. The nation became incorporated into the Soviet Union as the Estonian Soviet Socialist Republic. Estonia declared itself an "occupied territory", and proclaimed itself a free nation in March of 1990. During an abortive Soviet coup, Estonia declared its independence in September 1991.

An important slogan for Estonia is **"Eestlane olen ja eestlaseks jaan"** which can be translated as "I'm Estonian and will always be Estonian." This was the rallying cry of Estonians who engaged in the peaceful "Singing Revolution" of the late '80s that gained them independence from 50 years of Soviet occupation. This slogan is also the title of a popular song in Estonia.

Source:
Estonian Embassy, Washington D.C.

ETHIOPIA

———————•———————

Slogans in Ethiopia were quite dominant during the revolutionary government period of control over the nation,
(1974-91). One of the most interesting slogans launched
by the military government against the government of
Emperor Haile Selassie was

"ኢትዮ ቅድ : ትብይ ም: ያh : ም3 ም : ኤ ም"

meaning "Ethiopia first without bloodshed."

The army was afraid that the revolution would not be
accepted by the people if it was going to use violence
against the establishment. The emperor was overthrown
on September 12, 1974. A few months later about 60 dig-
nitaries of the monarchy including generals, nobles and
ministers were shot. The slogan speaking about no bloodshed stopped being heard in the media and was replaced
by others such as " meaning "Revolutionary Ethiopia or
death." With the end of military rule in 1991 and the
establishment of an elected government, slogan creation
declined sharply,

Source:
Embassy of Ethiopia

FINLAND

———————•———————

One of Finland's most treasured slogans is from the long time president of Finland (from 1956 to 1981) Mr. Urho Kekkonen. He, at the end of the 1950s spoke in the UN General Assembly and explained there the Finnish approach to world politics. His slogan was **"Suomi ei pyri toimimaan tuomarina vaan lääkärinä"**, or in English "Finland's aim is not to act as a judge but as a doctor." Since then this slogan has been used repeatedly and is still one of the most basic principles of Finland's foreign policy. It simply means that Finland can best give its contribution to international peace and stability by trying to act as a mediator rather than by condemning those who have been wrong and praising those who have been right. The latest evidence of this policy was Finland's central role in bringing peace to the war in Kosovo early in 1999.

Source:
Embassy of Finland.

FRANCE

During the period of the French Revolution, the National Convention opened on September 21, 1792. This governing body declared France a Republic. The Republic's official slogan was **"Liberté, Égalité, Fraternité"** which in English is "Liberty, Equality, Fraternity." The slogan, liberally interpreted, led several French feminists to make a bid for gender equality.

In 1791, Olympe de Gouges, an actress, playwright and revolutionary, composed *The Declaration of the Rights of Women and Citizenesses*. This work was a revision of *The Declaration of the Rights of Man* written to include women. She called for absolute political and legal equality, better education and equal rights in marriage. Gouges was a royalist, a defender of Louis XVI and an outspoken advocate of radical reforms. She ran afoul of revolutionary leaders such as Robespierre and Fouquier-Tinville. In the year 1793 Gouges was guillotined for being an enemy of the new regime. French society of the late 18th century was not prepared to pursue the implied ideals of their revolutionary slogan.

Sources:

Anderson, Bonnie S. and Judith P. Zinsser *A History of Our Own: Women in Europe from Prehistory to the Present Vol II* Harper-Perennial, New York 1988

Schama, Simon *Citizens: A Chronicle of the French Revolution* Vintage Books New York 1989

GERMANY

———————●———————

Even before the Kingdom of Prussia organized modern Germany (1871), political slogans were being used. King Frederick Wilhelm of Prussia in the mid-nineteenth century was quite concerned about the political unrest sweeping through many European powers. He wanted no unrest among his subjects and used this slogan to instruct his people, **"Ruhe ist die erste burgerflicht"** (Calmness is the first duty of a citizen).

Germany in World War I was typical of many nations involved in titanic struggles-it wanted to have God on its side. The German slogan was **"Gott sei mit uns"** (God be with us).

In the period shortly before and during World War II Germany took the prize for slogans. Joseph Goebbels (1897-1945) was the official propagandist of Nazi Germany. He spent great effort to persuade both Germans and non-Germans that Nazism was the irresistible wave of the future. He controlled radio programs, publications, motion pictures and the arts in both Germany and Nazi-occupied Europe. Goebbels set out to gain support for Nazi rule and tried to use words to build a powerful totalitarian state.

The slogans born from the Nazi propaganda machine were extensive and covered a multiplicity o topics. One of the early slogans was **"Deutschland Erwache"** which was a call for Germany to awake to the need for a new order, a new way of life. Slogans that were helpful in building support for Adolf Hitler, the Fuhrer (leader) were **"Ein Reich, ein Volk ein Fuhrer"** (One Nation, one People, one Leader). Another of this kind of slogan was **"Fuhrer befiel, wir folgen!"** (The leader commands, we follow!). This was often followed by another slogan **"Alle sagen Ja!"** (All say <u>Yes</u>!).

As the campaign of hate against the Jews got underway, such slogans as **"Deutschland Juden Frei"** (Germany free of Jews) and **"Deutsche! Wehrt Euch, Kauf nicht bei Juden!"** Germans! Protect yourselves, don't buy from Jews!) appeared. By the twisted logic of the Nazis the Jews were seen as a source of danger for Germans.

The Nazis tried to influence every aspect of life. It was seen as important to control women's behavior. The perfect German women formed an image that didn't include smoking cigarettes. In restaurants and cafes this slogan was often seen, **"Die Deutsche Frau raucht nicht."** (The German woman doesn't smoke.)

Nazi ambitions for conquest were illustrated by the slogan **"Heute gehort uns Deutschland und morgen die ganze welt."** (Today we have Germany, tomorrow the whole world,).

The young minds of the members of the Hitler Jungen (Hitler Youth) were fed a steady diet of slogans to turn young people into warriors. Hitler Youth leaders often had daggers, standard features of many Nazi uniforms, emblazoned with the slogan, **"Blut und Ehre"** (Blood and Honor). Another Hitler Jungen slogan was **"Wir Sterben fur Deutschland"** (We were born to die for Germany).

Slogans were even prepared for concentration and death camp inmates. At the gates to camp were slogans such as **"Arbeit macht Frei"** (Work makes you free) which was supposed to have a therapeutic effect on the prisoners' minds. Through devotion to work, prisoners would lose all cares and feel contented, or so the Nazis hoped. Even at the end when the Nazi cause was finished and the Russian army was about to take Berlin, one could see this slogan painted on walls by Nazi diehards, **"Berlin bleibt Deutsch"** (Berlin remains German).

There are few places or times in world history in which slogans were so heavily relied upon as instruments of propaganda.

Sources:
German Consulate, San Francisco for slogans from the mid-nineteenth century and for World War I

Herzstein, Robert Edwin and Editors of Time-Life Books *The Nazis* Time-Life Books Alexandria, Virginia 1980

GREECE

———————— ● ————————

Greece became a part of the Ottoman Empire in 1453. The Greek struggle to free itself from Turkish rule is known as the Greek War of Independence. The war started in 1821 and ended with Greece achieving independence in 1829. The slogan that best illustrates the spirit of Greece's struggle with the Turks is

" ΕΛΕΥΘΕΡΙΑ ΗΘΑΝΑΤΟΣ "

which means "Live Freely or Die."

Source:
Embassy of Greece

ICELAND

---•---

The motto (slogan) of the leader of Iceland's struggle for independence, Jon Sigurdsson, **"EIGI VIKJA"** (Never yield). Iceland's attempt to break free of Denmark was ended in a series of compromises. In 1901 limited home rule was won. In 1919 full home rule was achieved and finally in 1944 there was a restoration of the Republic of Iceland.

Source:
Embassy of Iceland, Washington D.C.

INDIA

India's national emblem is copied from a pillar built by Asoka, an ancient Indian ruler. Asoka ruled the Maurya Empire from about 272 BC until his death in 232 BC. Public announcements by Asoka have been found inscribed on great works and stone pillars throughout India. In these inscriptions, Asoka asked his people to treat one another with justice and mercy. He urged toleration of all peoples and beliefs. People and animals were not to be harmed unless it was unavoidable.

There are words of Asoka in Sanskrit beneath India's national emblem that state, **"Truth alone triumphs."** Sanskrit is the classical language that developed in India. It is the language of Hindu religion and culture. Linguists place Sanskrit within the Ind0-European language family which includes English and many other languages of Europe, Western Asia and Southern Asia.

Sources:
Consul General of India, San Francisco
World Book Encyclopedia, 1985

INDONESIA

Following the Japanese occupation of Indonesia (1942-1945), Indonesian nationalists, led by Sakarno and other leaders, declared independence on August 17, 1945. After an armed conflict, the Netherlands, the European nation that controlled Indonesia for centuries, ceded sovereignty on December 27, 1949.

A slogan that inspired Indonesian nationalists at this period was **"Merdeka"** (Freedom). The national motto of Indonesia is appropriately, **"Unity Through Diversity."** With over 13,000 islands, just keeping the nation together is of paramount concern to the Indonesian government. While most Indonesians are Moslem, there are Christian and Hindu followers as well as those who practice nature worship. There are major ethnic groups such as Javanese, Sundanese, Madurese, and Malay joined by numerous smaller ethnic groups.

Source:
Embassy of Indonesia, Washington, D.C.

IRELAND

———————●———————

One of the best known Irish slogans is **"Erin go Bragh"** which means "Ireland forever." It is a battle cry from the times of the ancient Irish warriors and has been included in much poetry and literature concerning Ireland's seemingly eternal struggle with its English neighbors.

In the 1170s, Norman barons from England seized Irish land. This was the first of a series of English incursions into Ireland. From the early days of the Normans, English control over the "Emerald Isle" (Ireland) weakened for some time but in 1541 a powerful King Henry VIII forced Ireland's Parliament to declare him king of Ireland. He introduced English laws in Ireland and tried to introduce Protestantism. Henry's son Edward VI and his daughters Mary I and Elizabeth I continued their father's policies throughout the 1500s. Mary seized land in some Irish counties and gave it to English settlers. Elizabeth I outlawed Roman Catholic services and executed a number of bishops and priests. Irish Catholics just dug in their heels.

In the late 1500s, a series of revolts broke out in Ulster, an area in Northern Ireland. The revolts were put down. James I continued the system of seizing Irish lands and giving them to English and Scottish Protestants. In time the Protestants became a majority in what would be called Northern Ireland.

In 1641 the Irish revolted against the Puritan leader of England, Oliver Cromwell. He crushed the revolt in 1649. He then gave away more Irish lands to English Protestants and deprived the Catholics of many political rights. When the Irish supported the Catholic James II in a struggle for the English throne, the defeat of their cause resulted in more land being taken from Irish Catholics.

By 1704 Catholics held only about 1/7th of the land of Ireland and were forbidden to purchase, inherit or even rent land. They were excluded from the Irish Parliament and the army. Their ability to practice Catholicism was restricted.

In the late 1800s more Irish people began to demand home rule. A rebellion arose on Easter Monday 1916. Fighting went on for weeks until the British army put it down. In 1919 fighting broke out between Irish rebels and British forces again. Finally, a treaty was signed in 1921 which led to a self-governing status for Ireland. Ireland declared itself a republic on December 21, 1948. Still conflict between Irish Protestants and Irish Catholics in Northern Ireland is just now looking like it might cool down as we enter the 21st century.

Source:
Morris, William and Mary *Morris Dictionary of Word and Phrase Origins* Harper and Row New York 1988

ISRAEL

———————•———————

The slogan ｜ n v ⊐ ٦ ۵ ٦ ⅁ w ｜ ｜ n ⅁ ⅁ ｜ P ｜ d e   means "Peace with security." The slogan was made popular after the signing of the Oslo accords.

There is strong sentiment behind the words of this slogan to reach a peaceful settlement with Palestinians, Syrians and other Arab groups such that the citizens of Israel will be safe and secure. Even before the state of Israel was established, Arabs and Jews living in what used to be called Palestine had several violent exchanges. The two groups fought bloody encounters in 1920, 1921, 1929 and 1936.

Israel was declared an independent state on May 14, 1948. The Arabs rejected the partition of Palestine. Egypt, Jordan, Syria, Lebanon, Iraq and Saudi Arabia invaded Israel but failed in their attempts to destroy the new nation. Later, in a six-day war that started on May 19, 1967, Egyptian forces reoccupied the Gaza Strip only to be repulsed and pushed back by Israeli forces. A settlement was eventually reached between Egypt and Israel.

In October of 1973 the Yom Kippur War began again threatening Israel. The peace settlement that was reached at the end of this war seems to have ended major hostilities among the Middle Eastern powers. Peace was disrupted however during the Persian Gulf War in early 1991. Iraq fired a series of scud missiles against Israel.

It is easy to understand the desires of Israelis to achieve the goals of the slogan "Peace with Security."

Source:
Embassy of Israel

ITALY

Slogans are not strangers to the Italian Peninsula. When Julius Caesar won a victory in 47 BC over Pharnaces II, King of Pontu, a slogan was born. **"Veni, Vidi, Vici"** (I came, I saw, I conquered) was Caesar's brief but important dispatch to the Roman Senate, reporting his victory at Zela in what is now northwestern Turkey.

In the 1840s, 1850s and into the 1860s many Italians tried to force the Austrians out of Italy and create a unified kingdom. The operatic composer Giuseppe Verdi joined his compatriots in displaying Italian nationalism. Several of his operas expressed patriotic sentiments. Italian patriots were pressing for Victor Emmanuel II, king of Sardinia, to unite all of Italy under his rule. Verdi, whose very name was taken to spell out Vittorio Emanuele Re D'Italia (Victor Emmanuel, King of Italy), provided the perfect slogan in the form of an acronym. The shouted slogan **"Verdi"** had a double meaning.

During Italy's Fascist period many slogans appeared. In October of 1922 the Fascists marched on Rome and King Victor Emmanuel III named Benito Mussolini premier of Italy. By 1925, Mussolini ruled Italy as dictator. He was called "Il Duce" (The leader).

Public works projects, a sense of social order and growing military strength won acclaim for the Fascists from many foreigners as well as Italians. Winston Churchill praised Mussolini as a great statesman.

The Fascists controlled the press and the radio. They used propaganda with great skill. Slogans were often stenciled on walls all over Italy. One that was reproduced widely was **"Mussolini ha sempre ragione"** (Mussolini is always right). Italians were urged to **"Credere, Ubbidere, Combattere"** (Believe, Obey, Fight).

Expansionist attitudes were illustrated by such slogans as **"A noi!"** (To us!) meaning to us goes the victory. In the Fascist invasion of France in June of 1940, the cry was **"Nizza nostra"** (Nice is ours). II Duce would often use the slogan **"Mare nostrum"** (Our sea) meaning that the British should be put on notice to stay out of the Mediterranean.

Italian anti-Fascists had their slogans too. When Italy invaded Ethiopia, those who opposed II Duce's move called out **"Down with the Fascist rape of the Ethiopian people."** In the same year that Mussolini conquered Ethiopia, 1936, he sent almost 70,000 men to help the rebels under Francisco Franco win the Spanish Civil War. Overly optimistic Italian anti-Fascists in Spain fought against Franco's legions with the cry **"Oggi in Spagna, domani in Italia"** (Today in Spain, tomorrow in Italy).

Post World War II Italy had some memorable slogans used by politicians. Giulio Andreotti, a Christian Democratic politician, served several terms as prime minister of Italy in the period from 1972 to 1992. He was one of Italy's most skillful and powerful political leaders of the post-war era. His statements were often infused with humor as when he made the often quoted remark **"A pensar male di qualcuno si fa peccato, ma stesso ci si ''Azzecca'!"** (To think ill of somebody is a sin, but very often hits the mark).

Sources:

Hoyt, Edwin Palmer *Mussolini's Empire: The Rise and Fall of the Fascist Vision* J. Wiley New York 1994

The new encyclopedia Britannica Encyclopedia Britannica, Inc. Chicago 1999

Adams, Henry and Editors of Time-Life Books *Italy At War* Time-Life Books Alexandria, Virginia 1982

Smith, Denis Mack *Mussolini's Roman Empire* The Viking Press New York 1976

JAPAN

The Japanese slogan **"fukoku kyohei"** literally means "Enrich the country and strengthen the military." It is a slogan of ancient Chinese origin used by the Japanese government in the Meiji period (1868-1912) to promote strategic industries and to strengthen Japan in relation to the western powers. During the Meiji period Great Britain, France, Germany, the Netherlands, the United States and Russia carried out imperialistic territorial, cultural and economic expansionist policies in eastern Asia, southeastern Asia and in the Pacific Ocean region.

Toward the end of the Edo period (1600-1868) these goals of strengthening Japan had been openly endorsed by Hashimoto Sanai, Sakuma Shozan, Yokoi Shonan and others. The leaders of the Meiji government similarly stressed "fukoku kyohei" because they believed that only a militarily strong Japan could effect the revision of the so-called Unequal Treaties and withstand the threat of Western imperialism.

The Meiji government instituted the Education Order of 1872, the Conscription Ordinance of 1873, and the Land Tax Reform of 1873 to 1881. It established government-operated factories and the Ministry of Public Works

(Kobusho), and promoted the dissemination of Western thought (bummei Kaika). The principal thrust of these policies was to enrich the country (fukoku) so that it could support a strong military (kyohei). Tremendous amounts of public capital were invested, with leadership centered in the Ministry of Public Works and the Home Ministry.

Of great importance were the military industries. The promulgation of the Conscription Ordinance was the beginning of a program of military expansion that came to include aggression on the Asian continent.

Source:
Embassy of Japan

L E B A N O N

Lebanon is a Middle Eastern nation on the eastern end of the Mediterranean Sea. Its neighbors are Syria on the East and Israel on the South.

An interesting and hopeful slogan from this country was designed to abolish sectarianism in an area scared by conflict among Jews, Moslems and Christians. In Lebanon the two major faiths are Islam and Christianity. The slogan in Arabic is "الدين اله و الوطن للجميع" which means "Religion is for God; the nation is for everyone."

Source:
Embassy of Lebanon

LUXEMBOURG

This Western European nation lies between Belgium in the West, France on the South and Germany in the East. With little more than a thousand square miles, it is one of Europe's smallest nations in land area.

Luxembourg was founded in 963 AD. The area has been ruled by many nations throughout its history. Burgundy, Spain, Austria and France have controlled the territory from 1448 to 1815. Luxembourg was created as a sovereign state by the Congress of Vienna in 1815. Later, it effectively saw its independence guaranteed on April 9, 1839 by the great powers of the era.

The slogan, which is prominently displayed today in Luxembourg City reads, **"Mir Wolle Bleiwe wat mir sin."** In English this reads, "We want to remain what we are."

Source:
Embassy of the Grand Duchy of Luxembourg

MEXICO

———•———

Mexico has many different slogans to choose from. The following statement is the most known world side **"El respeto al derecho ajeno es la paz."** This means "The respect for the rights of others is peace." When Benito Juarez was elected President in 1867, he expressed the following famous phrase in his address to the nation; "That, the people and the Government respect the rights of others. Between individuals and between Nations, the respect for the rights of others is peace."

Benito Pablo Juarez (1806-1872) was one of Mexico's greatest political leaders. He was elected president of Mexico in 1861. Juarez found the government in serious financial difficulty and stopped payment on European loans for two years. The French used this action as an excuse to kick Juarez out of office, invade Mexico and install Prince Maximilian as emperor.

Juarez directed the war against the French. In 1866, the United States virtually ordered the French out of Mexico. French troops withdrew. Maximilian was executed, and Juarez returned in triumph to Mexico City. Juarez again became president in 1867. He separated church and state, established religious toleration and altered the land system.

Source:
Mexican Cultural Institute, Washington, D.C.

NORWAY

———————•———————

In 1536 Denmark declared Norway a Danish province. After that date and for centuries thereafter Denmark was the major player in the running of Norwegian affairs.

After the Napoleonic Wars Sweden obtained Norway from Denmark. In September 1905, the Norwegians voted for independence from the Swedes. In November of 1905 the Norwegians approved Haakon VII, a Danish prince, as their king. He had a slogan **"Alt for Norge"** which means "All for Norway." This Danish prince wanted to show Norwegians he had broken his ties to Denmark and would give his all to his newly adopted nation. This slogan was used by his son King Olav V and is still being used today by King Harald V of Norway.

Source:
Royal Norwegian Embassy, Washington, D.C.

POLAND

———————●———————

A famous and popular slogan from Polish history is **"Za WOLNOŚĆ NASZĄ I WASZĄ."** It means "For our and your freedom."

This was the motto of Polish insurgents in the November Insurrection of 1830. Historically, after Napoleon's final defeat in 1815, Poland was again divided among Austria, Prussia and Russia.

A small, self-governing Kingdom of Poland was established under Russian control. Poles in the Kingdom of Poland rebelled against the Russians in 1830. The Russian Czar had abolished the Constitution and broke human rights. Polish soldiers felt that they were protecting the honor and freedom of all people managed by the Czar, i.e. Poles, Lithuanians, Russians, Ukrainians, etc. The war persisted about a year but Russia crushed the revolt and took away the little self-government that the Kingdom of Poland had.

Source:
Embassy of Poland

PORTUGAL

———————————•———————————

This slogan was very popular in Portugal after the 1974 Revolution. **"O povo unido jamais sera vencido"**, which means "A united people will never be vanquished." The slogan expressed the desire of the people of Portugal to never be under a dictatorship again.

Military officers overthrew the dictatorship in Portugal in 1974. They called their revolution the Armed Forces Movement. The movement abolished the secret police, restored rights to the people and established a provisional government to run the country. As part of the reforms, political parties were permitted for the first time since the 1930s. The new governments of Portugal began to withdraw from the nation's colonies. One of Europe's oldest empires retreated into the history books.

Source:
Portuguese Embassy Washington, D.C.

RUSSIA

———————●———————

There's quite a variety of Russian slogans. I have selected four that are well known in Russia:

1. The Russian poet Alexander Pushkin wrote about his native land, "The times were ripe with trouble broiling/In threatened struggles hared and stern/Young Russia had to try her strength/And slowly reach her full manhood/Beneath Great Peter's rule." The words Россия Молод meaning "Young Russia" are used to describe the reign of Peter the Great during which period Russia was transformed from a medieval state into a power on equal terms with the western powers.

2. "Могуча кучка" means "The Mighty Group" and refers to the circle of young Russian composers, including Rimsky Korsakov, Borodin and Musorgsky, who came to influence the whole development of musical life in Russia in the second half of the 19th century. The slogan is now used for any group of talented artists, writers, scientists, etc. who work in close collaboration.

3. "**Волдинская осень**" means "Boldino Autumn." This slogan is used to describe an exceptionally productive period in a writer's or artist's life. Originally the slogan was used with reference to a particularly fertile period in the creative life of Alexander Pushkin, the autumn of 1830, which he spent in the village of Boldino.

4. In 1917 a Bolshevik (Communist) slogan that struck a responsive chord in the hearts of many Russian People was **"Mir, Zyemlya, Khlep"** meaning "Peace, Land and Bread." World War I was a devastating experience for Russia. The battle deaths alone were approaching two million. Peasants wanted land that they could call their own and a full stomach which was too often a rare event as this conflict dragged on. The propaganda value of this slogan was inestimable.

Source:
Russian Cultural Center, Washington, D.C.

SAUDI ARABIA

———————•———————

The inscription on the flag of Saudi Arabia is the "shaha-da", the Moslem statement of faith. In Arabic the slogan is "There is no God but Allah, and Mohammed is the prophet of Allah." In Islam Mohammed is the mes-senger of the one God. Moslem (Muslim) is an Arabic word meaning one who submits to God. Islam is an Arabic word for submission.

The green flag of Saudi Arabia shows the white letters of the "shahada" emblazoned across it. The flag flies over a nation that occupies most of the Arabian Peninsula. The Islamic religious code is the law of the land. The country contains the holy cities of Islam-Medina, where the Mosque of the Prophet enshrines the tomb of Mohammed, and Mecca, his birthplace.

Source:
Crampton, William G. *Flags* Bloomsbury Books, London 1991

SPAIN

---•---

An unusual slogan from Spain is **"Plus Ultra"** which means "further ahead" in English. The slogan, which is on the coat of arms in Spain, had undergone a transformation. It is linked to the supposed existence of the two pillars of the Straits of Gibraltar in the mythical times of Hercules. He was the Greek hero who opened the Straits of Gibraltar thus joining the Mediterranean Sea and the Atlantic Ocean. Until the 15th century, the slogan used at the Straits of Gibraltar was **"non Plus Ultra."** This meant that there is not more land ahead. After the discovery and colonization of America by the Spanish kings, from 1492 on, the "non" word was removed from the slogan. This recognized the fact that new lands existed on the other side of the Atlantic Ocean. "Plus Ultra" are Latin words and as such are used even today.

Source:
Embassy of Spain, Washington, D.C.

SWEDEN

———————•———————

Although Sweden was neutral during World War II, Swedish authorities thought that people should be careful in talking to "strangers", i.e. foreigners. **"En Svenk Tiger"**, "Swedish Tiger", is a slogan symbolized by a picture of a striped blue and yellow tiger. The idea of keeping silent followed from the fact that tiger is a Swedish verb meaning to keep silent. The Swedish public was asked to keep quiet about anything they knew about the nation's defense.

Source:
Embassy of Sweden, Washington, D.C.

TRINIDAD AND TOBAGO

———————•———————

One political slogan in the history of Trinidad and Tobago is **"Discipline, Production, Tolerance."** These watchwords were given to the nation by its first Prime Minister, Dr. Eric Williams. He explained their significance in a speech to schoolchildren on the day before the country gained its independence on August 11, 1962.

"I have given to the nation as its watchwords, Discipline, Production, Tolerance. They apply as much to you, the young people, as to your parents. The discipline is both individual and national. The individual cannot be allowed to seek his personal ambition at the expense of our nation. We must produce in order to enjoy. Wealth does not drop from the skies for any individual or any nation. Reduce production, skylark on the job, take twice as long to do a job and make it cost twice as much-do any of these things and in effect you reduce the total amount available to be shared among the total number of people. Some of you have ancestors who came from one country. Some of you profess one religion, some another, others a third or fourth. You in your schools have, like the nation in general, only two alternatives-you learn to live together in peace, or you fight it out and destroy one another. The second alternative makes no sense and is sheer barbarism. The first alternative is civilized and is simple common sense."

Source:
Embassy of Trinidad and Tobago

TURKEY

Many of Turkey's most famous national mottos are from the founder of the modern Turkish Republic, Kemal Ataturk. One of his most famous remarks is **"Yurtta sulh, cihanda sulh"** meaning "Peace at home, peace in the world." Ataturk strove to bring peace, security and stability to his nation which put a damper on foreign adventures.

Kemal Ataturk (1881-1938) served as president of the Turkish Republic from 1923 until his death. He was a forceful leader and undertook a staggering number of reforms in Turkish society. He freed Turkish women and abolished such customs as the harem, the veil, the fez and polygamy. He introduced the Roman alphabet for the Turkish language, improved public education and eliminated corruption. He encouraged the development of banks and new industries.

Ataturk, a name given to him by the Turkish Assembly, means "Father of the Turks" and Kemal means "perfection."

Source:
Turkish Tourist Office, Washington, D.C.

UNITED KINGDOM

———————●———————

The United Kingdom of Great Britain and Northern Ireland is the official name for the country that many people incorrectly call England. Great Britain is a term that includes England, Scotland and Wales. England is the paramount section of this United Kingdom.

The slogans presented here are from early English history. These slogans are a source of bewilderment to many people because they are written in French. People may say, "Why are they written in French and not English?" The explanation begins with the William, Duke of Normandy, who invaded England in 1066. He defeated the Anglo-Saxon King Harold at the Battle of Hastings and became the first of several French speaking Norman rulers. Eventually, Norman French words merged with the Germanic vocabulary of the Anglo-Saxons to create what would become, over time, modern English. Before this merger took place, the English kings of Norman background used French for their mottos.

"Dieu et mon droit" is French for "God and my right" and is the motto of the Sovereign. The words were the countersign (military password) chosen by King Richard I before the battle of Gisors in 1198, meaning that he was no vassal of France, but owed his loyalty to God alone. The French were defeated in battle, but the password was not adopted as the royal motto of England until the time of Henry VI and has since been retained by his successors. The motto appears below the shield on the Royal Coat of Arms.

"Honi Soit qui mal y pense" is French for "Evil be to him who evil thinks." This statement appears on a garter which surrounds the shield on the Royal Coat of Arms. This garter symbolizes the Order of the Garter, an ancient order of knighthood of which the Queen is sovereign. The Order of the Garter was founded by Edward III in 1348 during the Hundred Years War with France. The motto may well have been directed at critics of the King's claims to the French throne; however, according to a tradition first recorded by Tudor chroniclers, the motto originated at a feast celebrating the capture of Calais in 1347. The King's mistress, the Countess of Salisbury, was mocked by courtiers for losing her garter during a dance, but Edward at once stepped forward and tied the blue ribbon around his own knee, uttering the motto as a rebuke and declaring that the Garter would soon be held in the highest esteem!

Source:
Foreign and Commonwealth Office, London

THE UNITED STATES OF AMERICA

———•———

Many political slogans in American history emerged from war and national expansion policies. Even before the Declaration of Independence was written in 1776, slogans appeared to rally support for confrontation with Great Britain. Virginia's Culpeper Minute Men (1775) had flags displaying such slogans as **"Liberty or Death"** and **"Don't Tread on Me"**. Also in 1775 the Continental Navy began using a red and white striped flag with a rattlesnake design displaying the slogan **"Don't Tread Upon Me."** At about this time the New England Bedford Flag bore the words **"Vinie aut Morire"** meaning "Conquer or Die".

In the War of 1812, Perry's flag bore the last words of James Lawrence, a hero of the war. Those words were **"Don't give up the ship"** and they became one of the most famous naval slogans in American history.

The concept that persisted in much of American foreign policy is given the name "Manifest Destiny". The expansion of America was seen as its obvious destiny. **"Fifty**

four forty or fight!" was a slogan of American expansionists seeking a northwards extension of the Oregon frontier. The slogan figured in the election of 1844 when land acquisition fever caught many Americans in its grip. The Oregon Controversy between the United States and Great Britain was settled by a compromise in 1846 which resulted in the border between British Colombia, Canada and the United States being drawn at the 49th parallel of latitude. President James K. Polk, who had his heart set on getting California from Mexico by purchase or conquest, didn't want to fight Mexico and Great Britain at the same time. A compromise with the British would allow Polk to focus on his expansion into Mexican territory. The War of 1847 between the United States and Mexico resulted in Mexico's defeat and the American acquisition of most of Mexico.

The Civil War (1861-1865) was the bloodiest most costly conflict in American history. About 620,000 soldiers died as a result of the war. Its effects on American society are still felt today as is seen in the debate over the flying of the Confederate battle flag in some places in the American South. On March 3, 1865, a three-cent copper-nickel coin was introduced with "In God We Trust" placed on it. Under the stress the Civil War produced on American thinking and feeling, **"In God We Trust"** and **"E Pluribus Unum"** (Out of many one) were featured slogans of the act of 1873 which was designed to revise the coinage laws.

There was a great revival of religious sentiment in America based on the horrendous suffering undergone by both the

North and the South. **"E Pluribus Unum"** was an appropriate slogan to use in an attempt to reunite the war torn nation. The motto **"In God We Trust"** was adopted in July of 1956 by the Congress of the United States as the official motto of the nation.

To many the Cold War was seen as pitting the godless atheistic Soviet Union against the God honoring United States. Americans, not unexpectedly, seemed to want God on their side.

At the end of the 19th century, a revolt in Spanish Cuba drew a strong response from the United States which favored having European powers leave the Western Hemisphere. To protect Americans in Cuba from the dangers of Spanish rioting in Havana, the battleship *Maine* was sent to Havana Harbor. The ship arrived there on January 25, 1898. On February 15, an explosion blew up the ship and killed about 260 persons on board. The outraged American public, roused by inflammatory newspaper articles, immediately blamed Spain for the explosion. **"Remember the *Maine"*** became a popular slogan of the ensuing war between Spain and the United States.

In the early period of World War I, (1914-1918) American sympathies were fairly pro-British. Anti-German feelings were inflamed by such things as the foolish Zimmermann note. With this note the Germans hoped to enlist Mexico to their cause with the promise of returning their lands lost to the United States.

Another thorn in the side of Americans was the German policy of unrestricted submarine warfare.

On April 2, 1917, President Woodrow Wilson called for war, stating to the Congress that **"the world must be made safe for democracy."** This became a national slogan during our participation in World War I.

On December 7, 1941, air and naval forces of Imperial Japan attacked Pearl Harbor in Hawaii. This brought the United States into World War II with the rallying cry **"Remember Pearl Harbor."**

Slogans have also appeared frequently in American political campaigns. There is a case where a slogan may have changed the political affairs of the nation. During his campaign for the presidency in 1884, James G. Blaine visited New York City. On the 29th of October at a large meeting of delegates assembled to meet with Mr. Blaine and offer their support - catastrophe struck! The group's spokesman was the Presbyterian clergyman Samuel D. Burchard. He declared that a vote for the Democratic contender for the presidency, Grover Cleveland, would be a vote for **"rum, Romanism and rebellion."** There were popular prejudices at the time that tied the Democrats with whisky (Irish drinkers), the power of the Roman Catholic Church and sympathies with the South in the Civil War. Some enemies of Blaine said that he was the author of the slogan. Roman Catholics were shaken by the statement. It is thought to be quite possible that this slogan denied Blaine the White House in a very close election.

Grover Cleveland became the 22nd President of the United States and the first Democrat to occupy that office since Abraham Lincoln. Incidentally, Cleveland's Republican detractors spread rumors that he had fathered a child out of wedlock. In political parades some Republicans pushed baby carriages through the streets shouting the slogan, **"Ma! Ma! Where's my pa! Gone to the White House, ha, ha, ha".**

American civil rights movements have come up with slogans over the years. In the mid to late 19th century a popular abolitionist as well as feminist slogan was **"Resistance to tyranny is obedience to God."**

Sources:
Crampton, William G. *Flags* Bloomsbury Books, London 1991

Stanwood, Edward *James Gillespie Blaine* Boston and New York 1908

Nussbaum, Arthur *A History of the Dollar* Columbia University Press New York 1957

Harper Book of Quotations Harper and Row New York 1988

Stanton, Elizabeth Cady *The Woman's Bible* Northeastern University Press Boston 1903

VIETNAM

———————•———————

In the history of the Vietnamese people there is a slogan which has inspired patriots. The slogan is written in gold plated characters and put on a granite wall. In Vietnamese it reads, **"Khong co gi quy hon doc lap tu do."** In English it reads, "Nothing is more precious than independence and freedom."

The Vietnamese people's struggle for independence goes back thousands of years in history. Vietnam was held by China from the 2nd century BC to AD 939. The country was a vassal state of China for some time. The Vietnamese defeated the forces of the invading Mongol ruler Khublai Khan in 1288 AD. Khublai Khan ruled the largest contiguous empire in history but he couldn't subdue these strong willed people.

In more recent history the imperialistic French began their campaign to conquer Vietnam in 1858 and brought it to a close in 1884 with the establishment of the protectorates of Tonkin and Annam in the North and the colony of Cochin-China in the South. A protectorate is defined as a relationship of protection and partial control assumed by a superior power over a dependent country or region.

Japan took over Vietnam from France in 1940.

Vietnamese nationalism developed under the guidance of Ho Chi Minh, Uncle Ho. This man began his drive for the independence of his country at the end of World War I when he was encouraged by the Fourteen Points announced by President Woodrow Wilson of the United States. Wilson's call for the "self determination of nations", seemed to be a plea for the end of colonialism. France and other imperialistic powers ignored the appeal. When Ho Chi Minh returned to his native Vietnam he vowed to devote his life to the cause of Vietnamese independence.

At the end of World War Ii the French tried to reestablish their control over Vietnam. From 1946 to 1954 the French carried on a major colonial war. During the struggle the slogan, **"Nothing is more precious than independence and freedom"** inspired many Vietnamese to make great sacrifices to achieve the goal of national independence.

Source:
Embassy of Vietnam, Washington, D.C.

ZIMBABWE

———————•———————

Zimbabwe is a nation in southern Africa. Its neighbors are Zambia to the North, Botswana on the West, South Africa on the South and Mozambique on the East. Most citizens of Zimbabwe belong to the Shona ethnic group known throughout the world for their outstanding sculpted art pieces. A Shona slogan from the Liberation War (1963-1979) **was "Zimbabwe Ndeye Ropa"** which means "Zimbabwe came out of blood."

In Zimbabwe's first universal-franchise election, April 21, 1979, Bishop Abel Muzorewa's United African National Council gained a bare majority of the black-dominated Parliament. A cease-fire was accepted by all parties on December 5. Independence as Zimbabwe was finally achieved on April 18, 1980.

Source:
Embassy of the Republic of Zimbabwe